Old Cottingham Remembered

by
Kenneth R. Green

HUTTON PRESS
1988

Published by the Hutton Press Ltd.
130 Canada Drive, Cherry Burton, Beverley
East Yorkshire HU17 7SB

Copyright © 1988
First published 1988
Reprinted 1989, 2000

Phototypeset, printed and bound by
Image Colourprint Ltd.,
Grange Park Lane, Willerby,
East Yorkshire HU10 6EB.

ISBN 0 907033 74 1

*This book is dedicated to the memory
of Councillor Leonard Thompson of Cottingham,
who did much and achieved a great deal
for Cottingham and its people.*

ACKNOWLEDGEMENTS

My thanks are extended to the following, for their assistance in the compilation of this book:

My wife, Mrs. Eileen M. Green, for her encyclopaedic knowledge of Cottingham and its people.
Mrs. E. Barker (daughter of Mr. H. J. Tadman).
Mr. Norman Bisby.
The late Mrs. Ellen C. Brace.
Messrs. Frith, Scott and Lilywhite.
Mrs. B. Gibson.
The Hull Daily Mail, for permission to use photographs.
Mr. John Markham, M.A.
Mrs. B. Worthington.
Mr. H. R. Wright.
Finally to all members of the Cottingham Local History Society and others who have contributed photographs.

Kenneth R. Green
Cottingham
October 1988

Special Note

Copyhold. Readers will see this term often used in the text. It is defined in the Standard Oxford Dictionary thus: "A kind of tenure in England of ancient origin: tenure of lands being parcel of a manor, at the will of the lord according to the custom of the manor, *by copy of the manorial court roll*". That is to say that the holder or tenant had no deeds, except that of acknowledgement of tenure in the manorial court rolls. No copyhold estate may be created at the present time.

CONTENTS

Page

1. Introduction 7

2. Church of St. Mary the Virgin 9

3. Notable Buildings and Houses 11

4. Street Scenes 49

5. Old Transport 83

6. Cottingham Personalities 86

Site map of Cottingham Village centre — Reproduction of map, drawn by the late John Whitehouse.

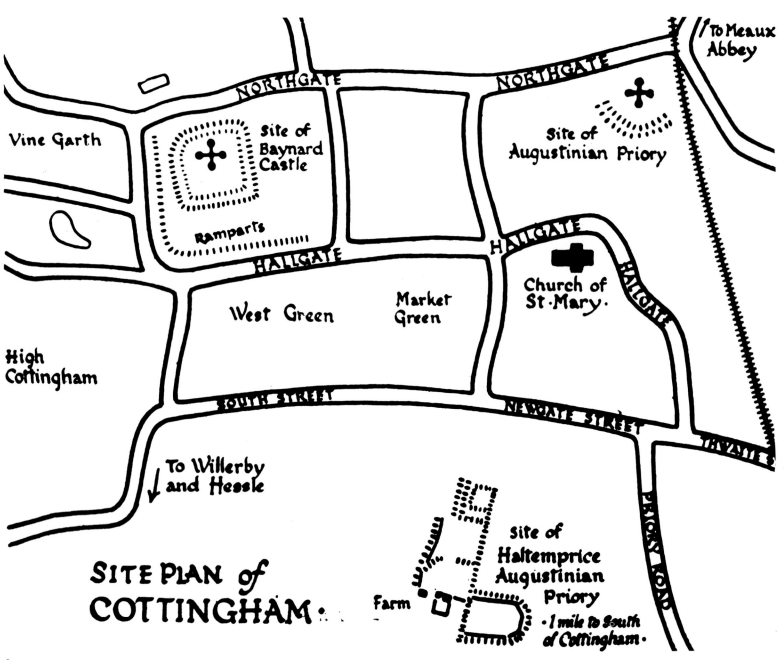

Vine Garth

Site of Baynard Castle

NORTHGATE

NORTHGATE

To Meaux Abbey

Site of Augustinian Priory

Ramparts

HALLGATE

HALLGATE

HALLGATE

Church of St·Mary.

West Green

Market Green

High Cottingham

SOUTH STREET

NEWGATE STREET

THWAITE S

To Willerby and Hessle

SITE PLAN of COTTINGHAM·

Farm

Site of Haltemprice Augustinian Priory

·1 mile to south of Cottingham.

PRIORY ROAD

Introduction

It has long been the proud boast of Cottingham folk that they inhabit the largest village in England; possibly an arguable statement, but an inspection of a map in the Victoria County History for the East Riding (Volume 4) shows that in 1600 the parish extended from Eppleworth Wood in the west to Hull Bank in the east, a distance of 7l/2 miles. The origin of the name Cottingham is doubtful, but the accepted explanation is that it signifies the settlement of Cotta's people; Cotta may have been a chieftain or possibly a Celtic goddess of somewhat doubtful origins.

The Domesday Book informs us that in 1086 Hugh, son of Baudry, with connections in Normandy, held 142/3 Carucates of land in Cottingham Manor and 2 Carucates at Pileford (modern Pillwoods), which had formerly belonged to the Saxon Gamel, son of Osbert, before the Norman Conquest. Eventually the manors passed to Robert de Stuteville, who forfeited them for his part in a rebellion against Henry I. They were restored to Robert's grandson (another Robert) during the reign of Stephen and remained in the de Stuteville family until 1241, when in the absence of male heirs the manor passed to Hugh Wake on his marriage to Joan, sole heiress. Hugh Wake died later in 1241 and Joan remarried, to Hugh Bigod (d.1266), but the manor passed to Joan's son Baldwin Wake on her death in 1276.

Cottingham still possesses impressions of Joan's seal showing her on horseback and claimed to be the first illustration of a woman riding side-saddle.

In 1320 Thomas Wake was granted a licence to build a monastery for Augustinian canons in a position to the south east of Northgate (in the area, now Station Road) but there arose legal problems concerning the land tenure and the monastery was re-established in 1324 at the hamlet of Newton, about one mile to the south of Cottingham and named "Alta Prise" or "Haulte Emprise", later corrupted to Haltemprice. The Wakes were also granted licences to fortify and castellate the manor house situated at the west end of Hallgate, and to be later known as "Baynard Castle".

It should be noted that the name "Hallgate" signifies the "gata" or street in which the hall or manor stands.

The Wakes retained the manor until the death in 1349 of Thomas Lord Wake without male issue, and it passed to his sister Margaret, dowager countess of Kent. On her death in 1349 Margaret's son, John Plantagenet, earl of Kent, assumed the estate as a barony together with the manor of Little Weighton and on his death in 1352 it passed to his sister Joan Plantagenet, better known as the "Fair Maid of Kent". Joan married twice, first to Thomas de Holand (d.1360) and then to Edward Plantagenet better known in later times as the "Black Prince". This association with the Plantagenets and the Crown was to be repeated in later times and accounts in part for the growing importance of Cottingham.

The manor passed to successive earls of Kent (via Joan's first marriage) until the death in 1408 of Edmund de Holand without male heirs. He was succeeded by four sisters, Joan, Margaret, Eleanor and Elizabeth; another sister also named Eleanor had a son, a minor, Edmund de Mortimer who was in wardship to Edmund de Holand's widow Lucy. This boy was liveried in 1413. It was at this point that the manor of Cottingham divided into four portions according to the marriages of the co-heiresses to their various lords, as Cottingham Richmond, Cottingham Sarum, Cottingham Westmorland and Cottingham Powis. A portion of the latter was granted to Richard Plantagenet, Duke of York in 1434. With the bitter struggle of the War of the Roses, by the end of the Plantagenet dynasty, the manor in all its parts had been assimilated to the Crown. By 1628 Powis, Richmond and Westmorland had been acquired by the grantees of the City of London as securities for a loan to the Crown. There followed a succession of owners through the following years until eventually it was split up and sold in lots by Francis Adrian Haworth-Booth (died 1952) who had lived at Haworth Hall, originally known as "Hull Bank House".

Cottingham has seen many changes since the early years of the last century, particularly in relationship to its rapidly growing neighbour Kingston-upon-Hull. The latter end of the eighteenth century and the finish of the Napoleonic Wars in 1815 eventually saw a growth in the economy of Hull and the development of shipping, business and banking. Successful businessmen took advantage of easy access to Cottingham using the new turnpike roads to build their stately Georgian houses on the outskirts of the village and Cottingham began to experience a new phase in its development. The expansion of the shopping areas in Hallgate began as the population increased to 1,927 in the 1801 census.

A period of development began at the turn of this century, halted by the war of 1914-1918. Following the post-war depression there was further development of the village and a new factor entered with the foundation of Hull University College and its buildings in 1928. Principal Arthur E. Morgan decided to acquire Thwaite House, formerly the residence of Lt. Col. Goddard, as a hall of residence for students, followed by the acquisition of Northfields House in Northgate. Cottingham's association with the academic world began with "Thwaite Hall", for women and "Needler Hall", for men.

During the Second World War from 1940-45 a site on Harland Way occupying part of the Grange estate was used as a camp for American soldiers and on its vacation it was bought by the University, which had obtained its charter as a full University by 1954, to house a new influx of students. The camp was eventually demolished to be replaced by an impressive campus of halls of residence known collectively as "The Lawns", which of recent years has also functioned as a Conference Centre during vacation times.

Despite its transition from a village to what in essence is a University town, with a population estimated in the region of 18,000, Cottingham has retained a great deal of its charm as a village community. Much that was old has been lost to make way for housing developments and shopping; a great deal more may have been lost were it not for the past policy of the University to acquire redundant Georgian villas and turn then into student houses. Sadly retrenchment in its funds may lead to a partial reversal of this policy as the University has to realise on its assets.

Cottingham too has its satellite communities at Castle Park and Bacongarth as it becomes a fashionable commuter zone for the city of Kingston-upon-Hull.

The village centre is full of bustle and energy, largely due to the corporate efforts of its traders and the re-creation of its ancient market (on Thursdays) dating back to the days of King John. An added attraction has been the splendour of its Christmas illuminations — the envy of its neighbours!

Through the ages, dominating the whole scene is the presence of the church of St. Mary the Virgin with its lordly tower which competes in splendour with the King and Queen of Holderness at Hedon and Patrington respectively. It was built arguably between 1316 and 1416 and is noteworthy for the beauty of its chancel, rebuilt by Nicholas de Luda in the Perpendicular style. Nicholas de Luda (Louth) was probably the most famous of Cottingham's priests and a favourite of Edward III. The advowson of the living was in the hands of the Black Prince via his wife Joan Plantagenet. That St. Mary's enjoyed a privileged position is shown by its collegiate status at that time and the incorporation of the Garter Knights arms in the glass of the chancel. Sadly all this glass together with the mediaeval glass of the nave was wantonly destroyed in the Civil War. St. Mary's suffered also to some extent at the hands of the Victorian restorers; the priest's room over the south porch was removed by the Reverend C. Overton, who also lifted the nave floor, thereby shortening the nave pillars, with effective partial loss of their bases. A happier reconstruction was a later replacement of the simple chancel roof by the existing fine hammer-beam construction.

In present times much is owed to the untiring efforts and energy of the present incumbent the Reverend Canon T. Grigg in maintaining the fabric and well being of the church. This pictorial record of Cottingham has only been made possible by the wealth of pictures available and the main task has been one of selection.

In particular we are all indebted to the zeal of an early Cottingham photographer, Mr. H. J. Tadman, postmaster and registrar at the turn of the century. Other commercial pictorial cards, the vogue of the times, were produced by the firms of Messrs. Frith, Scott and Lilywhite.

Church of St. Mary the Virgin

Cottingham parish church, dedicated to the Blessed Virgin Mary, was built between 1316 and 1416, with later additions including relieving arches in the tower structure and the Georgian pinnacles on the tower. The rectors of the church date from the twelfth century, which would appear to suggest an earlier building of which no trace has been found, although some of the stone may have been re-used. The chancel is later than the nave and as the former would be expected to predate the nave, since it contains the altar, it is probable that the original chancel was replaced by a newer structure. Since the chancel is in the Perpendicular style and the nave in the flamboyant decorated style it is almost certain that the present structure was started in 1374 by Nicholas de Luda only fifty years on from the original building. As it is highly improbable that the original chancel had already decayed to the extent requiring replacement, we must assume that a grander structure was envisaged, because of the growing importance of St. Mary's. This is borne out by the inclusion of the arms of the Garter Knights in the chancel glass, especially those of the Black Prince.

A reproduction of a plate from the "Gentlemen's Magazine"
dated December 1797 showing the Mark Kirby free school and
a portion of the old workhouse.

A view of St. Mary's from the west end (c.1910) showing the circular clock faces (on all sides of the tower) which replaced the single earlier octagonal face on the west side only.

A south west view of the church in 1844 by Thomas Spenceley showing the priest's room above the south porch and the vertical sundial — both removed by the Revd. C. Overton.

Noteworthy Buildings of Cottingham

The Free School

This school bears the words "Mark Kirby Free School A.D. 1712" on the archway above the door, which is not strictly correct, for although the bequest for its foundation was in Mark Kirby's will by 1712, he did not die until 1718. The school and schoolmaster's house were adjacent to the old workhouse and are illustrated in the old print of St. Mary's from the "Gentlemen's Magazine" of 1779.

William Hardy was schoolmaster in 1784 and when the Overseers of the Poor tried to eject him from the schoolhouse, he brought a legal action in the courts at York and won his case, with £600 in costs awarded. The church hall, formerly known as "Arlington Hall", occupies a part of the original site of the workhouse.

Ivy House c.1910.

Ivy House (demolished)

A more modern name for this rather quaint old house; with its hipped roof of rough stone tiles and rear roof of local pantiles, it stood amidst the gravestones of the old churchyard. It was demolished in 1974 to make way for the new rectory, which replaced the former building on the opposite side of Hallgate.

The older directories make it difficult to pin-point former residents as it is described merely as "churchyard". It is likely that Samuel Watson, F.R.C.S., surgeon, was there in the 1870's and in 1892 (Bulmer's directory) Robert Garton. William Robinson, florist, lived there in 1905 and on his death the house was occupied by his unmarried daughters, the last inhabitants. One of these daughters had been a nurse in South Africa and returned here on retirement.

The new rectory on the site of Ivy House.

A view of the old rectory.

The Old Rectory, Hallgate

This rectory was built for the Revd. C. Overton in 1847 after the original house had been pronounced as being "unsuitable for its purpose". The architect was William Richardson; the churchwardens' accounts show that the cost was £1065 less £155 allowed for materials salvaged from the old building.

In 1973, the church acquired Ivy House in the old churchyard and this was demolished shortly afterwards to make way for a new rectory, built in 1974. The old rectory was demolished in 1976 and the extensive grounds used to build Hallgarth Old Peoples' Home and the new school for infants. Before its total demolition, the elaborate portico and door-case were removed and built into the new rectory.

No. 140 Hallgate

Sometimes referred to as "the old rectory", there is no evidence that it was ever used as such, although it was possibly used as a residence for assistant clergy. The placing of the old sundial, removed from the south porch of the church by the Revd. C. Overton, in this building supports this view. The shop shown in this picture was owned in pre-war days by Miss Hannah Fairbank and in post-war times by Mrs. Lena Tranmer. The premises to the left, a small wool shop, were used pre-war by Mr. Leonard Briggs, joiner, and an upstairs room to the rear was a meeting room for the Liberal Party. The building was taken down completely in the early 1960's and rebuilt in its present form, still incorporating the old sundial. This view shows Mrs. Tranmer's shop in 1956.

In the 1890's with the Kirk family in residence as farmers and market gardeners.

The Manor House

This is the oldest inhabited dwelling in the village and second only to St. Mary's as the oldest existing building; a genuine timbered structure, internal inspection reveals the original daub and wattle infill. It stands on the mound originally occupied by Baynard Castle, the fortified manor house built by the de Stutevilles.
William de Stuteville was granted a licence to build and eventually fortify a castle at the west end of Hallgate facing West Green and it was probably a simple wooden structure, surrounded by a wooden palisade; the main reliance on safety was placed on the extensive earthworks.
There were inner and outer moats (c.f. Leland's itinerary) surrounding the earth mound; traces of these moats still exist and it is probable that the existing mound is much smaller in height.
Leland, in the 25th year of King Henry VIII's reign was given

"a most gratius commission to peruse and diligently to serche al the Libraries of Monasteries and Collegies of this . . .

Reaulme, to the intente that the Monumentes of auncient Writers as welle of other Nations, as of this . . . Province mighte be brought owte of deadely darkenes to lyvely lighte".

This was the commission responsible for Lelands itinerary;

"geven of him as a Newe Yeares Gyfte to King Henry the VIIII in the XXXVII Yeare of his Raygne"

(1546 A.D.) Leland describes his visit to the site of the castle thus:-

"Entering into the South Part of the great Uplandisch Towne of Cotingham, I saw wher Stutevilles Castelle, dobill dikid and motid, stoode, of the which nothing now remaynith. The landes of this Signiorie and Lordship greatly privilegid cam of later tymes by division ynto 4. Partes, wherof now a late the King had one Part, the Countess of Saresby another, the Erl of Westmerland the 3. and the Lord Pops the 4. At this Tyme the King hath al, saving the Lord Pops part"

This is a direct confirmation of the partition of the manor, and the

In the 1960's a picture of dereliction.

The new frontage after renovation, with the addition of a porched structure, which does not detract from the original "essence" of the building.

phrase, "wherof now a late the King" must refer to acquisition by a previous monarch during the Wars of the Roses.

Leland continues in direct reference to the present structure;

"𝔄t this present 𝔗yme be 4. sundry meane fermers 𝔥ouses, as one for eche of the 4. 𝔏ordes withyn the 𝔠astelle 𝔊arth".

These four houses have obviously in modern times been thrown into one cottage.

The pictures selected here show the manor house:

An early photograph dating about 1910.

Southwood Hall

This 17th century house of the Bacchus family is regarded as the third oldest building and the second oldest inhabited house in Cottingham.

Legend has it that Charles I stayed here after his ill-fated attempt to enter the town of Kingston upon Hull in April 1632, when he was refused entry by Sir John Hotham. Despite some window changes it remains substantially intact, although almost completely encapsulated in a modern estate on Burton Road.

In 1764 it was acquired by a Hull merchant, Samuel Watson, and after his death in 1778, his widow Frances remarried, to the Reverend John Simpson of Bath, who sold the house to John Wray of Hull. It remained in the Wray family from 1811 until 1867 and although there is no evidence that they occupied it, there has been a suggestion that Thomas Thompson, Hull banker, may have lived there for a time. Daniel Dalby senior, appears there in Kelly's directories up to his death in June 1882 aged 91 years.

Brian Lazenby of the Railway Inn is listed in Kelly's directory of 1922 as also of "Southwood Hall Farm" and it has remained in the Lazenby family up to recent times.

A more modern photograph of the 1960's.

Daniel Dalby in his wheelchair c.1880.

The castle as reproduced from a very ancient photograph — one of the oldest known of a
Cottingham scene, predating 1860.

Cottingham Castle

In 1793, following the enclosure of open-field land to the west of Cottingham village, a Hull banker, Thomas Thompson purchased 54 acres of land on a rising site and built an ornate castellated mansion, which was to become known as "Cottingham Castle"; not to be confused with the ancient manor house in Hallgate known as "Baynard Castle". The mansion was built between 1814-1815 on a promontory (now occupied by a modern hospital) to become known as "Castle Hill". Thompson and his family lived here until his death in 1828, when he was succeeded by his elder son Col. Thomas Perronet Thompson. Perronet Thompson never actually lived there and it was tenanted first by George and Edmund Coulson until about 1851 and later by J. B. Barkworth Esq., until May 1861 when it was totally destroyed by fire. The Revd. Charles Overton records this event in the closing pages of his "History of Cottingham" published in 1861. Of this castle the only remains are those of the tower "folly" on top of Castle Hill, the ornate gateway being dismantled and removed during extensions to the hospital which now occupies the site.

The "folly" on Castle Hill c.1910; still in existence.　　　The Gateway; demolished in the 1960's.

Haltemprice Priory and Farm

In 1320, Thomas Wake obtained a licence for the foundation of a Priory for nine Augustinian canons to be built on a site in Northgate (in the area near Station Road) and work was commenced in 1322. By 1324 it was discovered that there were legal problems about land tenure and before extensive building had got under way the Priory was refounded at the hamlet of Newton about one mile to the south of Cottingham. The new foundation received the name "Alta Prisa" (Norman-French "Haulte-Emprise"), which

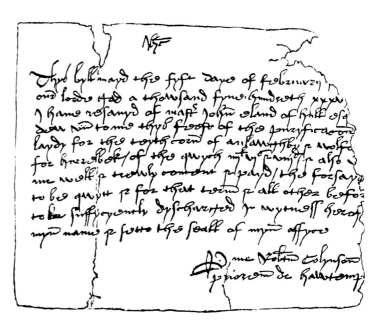

Ihc
Thys byll mayd the fyft daye of february [in the year of]
our lorde god a thowsand fyue hundreth xxxv [witnesseth that]
I haue resauyd of mast John eland of hull esq . . . .
dew vnto me thys feest of the puryficac'on [of our blessed]
laydy for the teyth corn of anlawghly & wolf [erton] . . .
for hurrelbek, of the qwych iiij vj & viij, & also . . . .
me well & trewly content & payd, the forsayd . . . .
to be qwytt & for that term & all other befor . . . .
to be suffycyently dyscharged   In wytness hereof . . . .
myn name & sette the seall of myn offyce

P' me Rob't'm Colynson
priorem de hawtemp [rice]

Document signed by Robert Colynson.

The great seal of the Priory.

can be rendered as "High Endeavour".

Henry VIII suppressed the foundation in 1536 and in the inventory of goods were included "an arm of St. George" and "a girdle belonging to the Blessed Virgin".

The last prior was Robert Colynson and the illustration shows an account bearing his signature.

Haltemprice Farm on or near the site of the Priory was probably built from stone derived from the ruins and is situated near a footpath running from Willerby to Cottingham. Nearby runs a spring of fresh water known as "Lady Well" in which the renowned local botanist Harrison discovered the rare diatom now known as "Fragillaria Harrisonii" — aptly described as a microscopic plant jewel of cruciform shape!

Haltemprice Farm.

Kingtree House from the east facing side.

Kingtree House (King Street South) — demolished

In the 1750's Samuel Watson junior, Hull merchant, acquired several small holdings, copyhold of the Rectory manor lying to the east of Market Green and had this house built on the estate. Arthur Young included Kingtree House in his visitations of Yorkshire in 1769 and declared the house and grounds as "well worth seeing". Watson died in 1778 and the house passed to his widow Frances, who sold it to Joseph Sykes, Hull merchant, in 1789. On Sykes' death in 1805, it passed to Nicholas Sykes (d.1827) and then to Joseph Shepherd, physician and surgeon from Kirby Moorside (North Yorkshire) in 1829. He died in 1832 and the trustees of his estate sold it to Dyas Lofthouse, Hull merchant in 1845.

W. H. Heap Hutchinson was there in 1892, but had moved to Cottingham Hall by 1900.

The Bilton family (Cyril F. W. Bilton) lived there until the early 1960's when the house was demolished to make way for a block of shops facing the Civic Hall and Finkle Street.

The gardens and tennis court overlooking the church, now part of Kingtree Avenue.

The west side on King Street facing Finkle Street.

Cherry Garth (earlier Beck Bank House)

This house had seen many changes before its final demolition in 1984. Built in the early 1700's it was bought in 1736 by John Chambers, Hull merchant, and it passed to his son John, officer of marines, who in turn bequeathed it to Anne Ringrose and Deborah Rickard. In 1776 the estate was divided between them, with Deborah taking the house. Her husband John Rickard died in 1812, passing the house to his son Thomas, who bequeathed it in 1817 to Anne Rickard, who had married Dyas Lofthouse, Hull merchant. Lofthouse owned the house until his death in 1876, but he had it completely rebuilt in 1866, with Dutch style gables.

The house was occupied by the younger John Chambers for a time and by John Lambert as tenants in the late 1700's and later by John and T. M. Rickard. In 1820 it was occupied by James Dean, Vicar of St. Mary's, and in 1831 Lord Henry Smith lived there. The Lofthouses lived there from about 1836 to 1845 and in 1848 army officer Charles Teale lived there, and by 1879 Lofthouse's widow was in residence. Walter Owbridge, lung tonic manufacturer, was there in the 1890's followed by Henry W. Franklin in the early 1900's, whose widow lived there in 1909. The Hildyard family were the last family occupants from the 1920's until the outbreak of the Second World War. It was during their occupancy that the large glass conservatory, adjoining Lynngarth Avenue, was used by Cottingham Roman Catholics prior to the building of Holy Cross Church in Carrington Avenue. In later years the house was converted into flats and demolished in 1984. The site is now occupied by custom built flats, still using the name "Cherry Garth".

Cherry Garth in the 1960's.

Bridge House (Newgate Street) - demolished

This cottage was formerly on a corner site at the junction of Beck Bank and Newgate Street. The sole remains are the foundations of a brick wall which dipped down into the now filled-in beck and the site has become a small leisure garden.

It was acquired by Caius Thompson, Hull merchant, in 1810, who probably renovated it, and it passed to his widow Mary c.1841. Thompson lived there from 1810, but by 1839 it was occupied by Mary Chapman. Another possible occupant could have been George Wells, Hull merchant, in 1851.

The last occupant was Miss Fanny Foster from about 1900, and the house was demolished in 1935.

Bridge House c.1925 — the only known view.

Snuff Mill House and Snuff Mill

This mill, more correctly designated South Mill, was one of the two important mediaeval watermills of the village. The other mill in Northgate, North Mill, was fed by Cottingham beck on its way from Millhouse Woods, via Beck Bank to Newland. Its primary function, like that of North Mill, was to grind corn, but it was rebuilt by William Long of Driffield in 1722 and it was used as a paper-mill until 1755, when it was bought by William Travis, Hull tobacco merchant, who used it to grind snuff. Travis built Cottingham Hall in the grounds and Snuff Mill became the property of the Hall owner in future years. Samuel Bolton in 1823 used the mill for making worsted cloth and later it was used by the Cottingham oil press cloth company for making oil press bagging cloth. The mill fell into disuse, but the house was tenanted by William Robinson, market gardener in 1900 and later he shared the tenancy.

The millhouse is still occupied, but the mill itself was demolished in the 1930's, showing only the mill race entry and parts of the mill wall in the garden of the house. The leet and mill arch disappeared in the 1960's when the beck was culverted and filled in.

H. Roper Spencer's drawing of 1750, showing the millrace.

SNUFF MILL HOUSE
COTTINGHAM 1750

H. ROPER SPENCER

Interior of the mill
c.1900.

Moving the supplies of jute for the
making of press cloth.

Cottingham Hall (demolished)

Thomas Travis, Hull merchant, in 1755 purchased Snuff Mill and built Snuff Mill House as a residence in 1760. By 1795, wanting a finer house, he built Cottingham Hall on the estate, with a sweeping drive to Thwaite Street. A fish pond ran across the rear of the house, flowing via a weir into Cottingham Beck. Tickell in his History of Hull (1797), who would see it soon after its completion, described it as "one of the chief houses in Cottingham...". William Henry Heap Hutchinson resided there in 1872, but left to live in Kingtree House in the 1890's and returned to Cottingham Hall by 1900.

The Hall was demolished in 1935, making way for housing development. Remnants of the building and the pathway over the fish pond to the snuff mill still remain together with the name "Hall Walk".

House frontage.

Rear of house.

Cottingham Hall. Bridge over the fish pond.

Cottingham House.

Cottingham House (demolished)

Not to be confused with Cottingham Hall, this house was the property of the Bacchus family and was bought by James Milnes, Hull merchant, in 1744. After Milnes' death in 1750, his widow Alice sold it to Jervas Scrope and Samuel Watson, junior, Hull merchant, in 1753. Watson died in 1778 and it was bought in 1786 by Hull merchant, Richard Moxon, who died by 1799, when it passed to son Richard William Moxon. In 1823 this son was bankrupt and the Commissioners in bankruptcy sold it to Mary and Elizabeth Hammond of Hull. In 1824 Mary Hammond sold it to Stephen Gee, Hull merchant, and on his death in 1841 it passed to his son, Joseph Gee, who died in 1860. By 1892 Gee's widow no longer appears in the directories and a new occupant, Henry Wilson, is in residence, followed by son George Wilson in 1897. J. J. Bickersteth and Lady Bickersteth, two well known Cottingham characters, lived there until 1925, to be followed by the Misses Rollitt. These two ladies were the last inhabitants until eventually the house was demolished in the early 1970's to be replaced by a modern dwelling.

Oakdene

Built by John Hill, Hull merchant, on 9 acres of land off South Street in 1816. He died in 1820, and the house passed to his son John, a solicitor, who let it to George Codd, Town Clerk of Hull; he was there in the 1830's and became one of the foremost citizens of Hull. The Codd family produced three generations of sons who were Town Clerks of the City.

The house was demolished in the 1960's to make way for a housing development, named "Oakdene" after the house.

"Oakdene" estate and the house.

Rydale (Villa), 146 Hallgate

This photograph shows Rydale in its original form as a small but elegant townhouse on a site purchased by Appleton Bennison, Hull builder in 1806. On his death in 1830 his executors sold the house to John James, Hull shoemaker, who sold it in 1839 to William C. Colbeck, a Hull solicitor. In turn the house was occupied by a Cottingham gardener; Samuel Bromby, watch-maker; and John James; followed by the Colbeck family. During the 1930's Mrs. Pye lived there and afterwards the house was radically altered, with the removal of the Georgian sash windows, bays being built out from the frontage. In its modern guise as the National Westminster Bank it is altered beyond recognition; the only clue in this picture is given by the appearance at the extreme left of the photograph — the Hallgate Methodist Church.

Rydale c.1910 in its original form.

Hallgate House

This house would not be recognised today having suffered many indignities in its transformation from a very fine townhouse, first to a Co-operative store and very recently into a multiple shop unit. Its street entry was in Hallgate, where the carriages would draw up to its elegant railings and portico, but the main frontage faced south to Finkle Street, with extensive gardens. It was built by John Wray in 1779 on land copyhold to Cottingham Richmond manor. It is best known as the home of the Paynes, Hull solicitors, who lived there for many years.

North face of Hallgate House, Hallgate entrance c.1910.

South side facing Finkle Street, showing members of the Payne family.

34

The White House, off Hallgate, with its stables

Originally known as Hallgarth House, it is now known as "White House". It stands on a small road, leading to the Manor House, which originally went through the castle grounds into Northgate. The White House was built about mid 18th century and was acquired by William Ringrose, Esq., in 1770. It remained in the Ringrose family for many years including John, Hull merchant (1820's), William (1830's) and Thomas (1841). It is however during this century best remembered for its association with the Throup family, acknowledged as leading breeders of Hackney Carriage horses. The old stable block still stands but its future preservation is extremely uncertain due to the pressure of development on the castle area. The property has been on the market recently following the death of the last Throup in residence.

White House.

Stable block.

Westfield House, Baynard Avenue

View from West Green c.1900.

This house stands at the junction of Baynard Avenue, Finkle Street and Hallgate, opposite Cottingham's oldest green known as West End.

Formerly a very fine Georgian House, with later additions it has lost much of its former glory and is now split between a country club and a restaurant.

The extensive gardens, rolling lawns and trees have disappeared to make way for a drab car park and a sauna house replaces the old stable block.

It was built by William Hall about 1778 on land copyhold of the Richmond manor. It was well known for its occupancy by the Lambert family until the turn of this century; probably the most important being the Revd. Canon Malet-Lambert associated with a famous Hull school, which bears his name. The Lamberts were followed by the Grotrians, best known for their association with the Hull Daily Mail. The Grotrians gave a debased version of their name to the nearby Dene, known colloquially as "Grote's Wood". During the two years 1937-1939 it was used by the University College of Hull as a hall of residence for students until the outbreak of the war. The magnificent gardens, which included a tennis court, lily pond and wishing well, have long since gone, as have the fine selection of Coalbrookdale fireplace grates. The central chimney stacks, however, still retain their distinctive cast iron chimney pots from Coalbrookdale.

Rear of the house showing part of the gardens c.1910.

Wishing well, with University students 1938.
1) Fenton G. Whelan 2) Roland Errington 3) Frank Walker 4) Ken Green.

George Knowsley and Cottingham Grange

George Knowsley, one of Cottingham's most influential figures, purchased a property from John Lambert, Hull merchant, at the west end of Northgate. It is conjectured that this property was on land now in the grounds of the University's Lawns Campus west of No. 282 Northgate. Knowsley, describing himself in 1787, as "of Cottingham", began in masterful fashion to alter this aspect of Northgate. He purchased the northern side of the Manor House estate and incorporated it into his own gardens, closing the old road into Hallgate. To compensate, he put through George Street (named after himself!), and he also moved Park Lane entrance to its present position near Park Row. Ironically the University has driven a new road for traffic through the Lawns campus in approximately the same position as the old lane! Knowsley now purchased a 9 1/2 acre site copyhold of the Richmond manor on adjoining land on Harland Way and by 1802 had built the Grange, demolishing his previous house at the same time. In 1806, in William Smith's "Old Yorkshire" Vol. 4, he is listed as Captain of Militia — strength 140 men. He died in 1809 and the Grange passed to his son George who sold it in 1828 to Robert Gleadow. In 1831 it was acquired by the Raikes, Hull bankers, and by 1838 it was occupied by George Codd, Hull solicitor. On Codd's death the house and estate was sold to William Ringrose, who owned much land in the area, extending the total estate to 565 acres. It remained in the possession of the Ringrose family until sold by the executors, by auction on March 25th, 1930. It was demolished by about 1936 and the gardens remained derelict until developed post-war. During 1939-45 it was an American soldiers' camp, but after 1956 a school was built on the site of the house and the soldiers' camp used as temporary residences for University students, before final development as a campus known as "The Lawns".

A picture of the Grange, probably during the occupancy as a tenant, of John Broadley Harrison-Broadley, who lived there from about 1912-15 until he moved to Welton House on the death of his father, Henry Broadley Harrison-Broadley. A gathering of the Holderness hunt is pictured here.

Another view of the Grange from the rear.

Park House c. 1910, with three of the household and a bicycle.

School.
E. Yorks

Park House

This house was copyhold in part to both Richmond and Sarum manors and appears to have been built for the widow of Benjamin Clegg, Alice Clegg. It is possible that Benjamin was the dissenting clergyman of that name. Eventually the house passed to Thomas Wilson, Hull merchant, who was to become famous as the founder of the largest world shipping line. He converted the house into a mansion, later to be occupied by David Wilson Esq., J.P. in the 1890's. In later years it became a private school, and it was demolished in 1935 to make way for a row of houses, and the grounds became the King George V playing fields. Within the last year (1987) a multi-coloured sports pavilion has been erected together with a bowling green with synthetic plastic grass!

In later years as a private school.

House shortly before demolition 1962, rear facing the extensive garden.

No. 150 Northgate; later "Northgate House"

This fine small Georgian house, copyhold of Sarum manor, was owned by William Green, school master, in 1839 and passed to J.W. Burstall, Hull merchant, in 1858. The Ringroses of Cottingham were here for a time, but the most remembered occupant was Dr. Arthur Tinley Sissons, a true Cottingham character. He was the last owner and on his death the house was put up for auction, but was compulsorily purchased by the Haltemprice Council in 1962 and the house demolished to make way for development of an executive type housing estate. Dr. Sissons' name is however perpetuated by the naming of "Tinley Close". A block of flats rise where the house stood and still bear the name "Northgate House".

View of the house, similar aspect, at a greater distance showing the ballroom at the side, later used as a private kindergarten school.

View of Needler Hall from Northgate.

"Northfields", (earlier Northgate House)

Now known as Needler Hall, University Hall for students, this house was earlier known as "Northgate House", before becoming "Northfields". Copyhold of Sarum manor it was built soon after 1780, but was extended by a new block facing the garden by 1820. In 1825 it belonged to George Ringrose and passed to the heirs of John Parker in 1831. It belonged later to Joseph Armstrong, chemist and druggist in 1845, and he disposed of it to Benjamin Rayner, gent. of Cottingham, who sold to Thomas Ringrose in 1847. Occupants included Edward Thompson, Hull merchant, and Richard Tottie. Between 1825 and 1834 it became a private mental asylum run by Joseph and Catherine Taylor. Later occupants were Thomas Dyson, Joseph Armstrong and Thomas Ringrose who returned with four servants in 1851.

41

North Mill

North Mill as seen here was a combined wind and watermill which had mediaeval origins as a watermill, fed by the northern end of the same beck which worked South Mill (Snuff Mill) on the other side of the village.

The windmill of typical East Yorkshire design with ogee cap, similar in style to the existing mill at Skidby, was built to operate the grindstones when water was low. The mill eventually ran with two sails and when reduced to one sail a steam engine was used for a time, but the mill was demolished by about 1900. The mill was last owned by the Needham family, and after demolition the small miller's cottage to the left of the mill remained in occupation by tenants until its demolition c.1935. Traces of the foundations and mill race existed through the middle years of this century and the beck flowed on under Northgate, across Alma nurseries and via Beck Bank into Snuff Mill Lane. With the development of Mill Beck Lane and in conjunction with the deep drainage scheme, the whole of the beck from this point to the boundaries of Hull was culverted. At the end of the 19th century the beck at this point was deep and wide enough to take a rowing boat, but the building of the waterworks in the Millhouse Woods area lowered the water table considerably.

Mill in 1884, possibly Isaac Needham in the doorway.

Mill about 1890, operating with two sails only.

Mill shortly before demolition, with only one sail. Mill cottage is seen to the left.

No.50 Northgate and Greystones from a water-colour by Alec Wright, local artist, who was born in Northgate.

Greystones (No.46 Northgate) and Cottages nearby

For many years, until the mid 1960's this portion of Northgate from the mill lane to the railway crossing preserved many of the essentially rural aspects of the village, with a rather imposing Georgian villa set amongst a cluster of cottages.

The name "Greystones" is somewhat inappropriate and also somewhat modern. Probably its best remembered occupant was Dr. James Galt, Hull physician and surgeon, but this house of unknown date (probably late 18th century) was built for William Lee. It has seen many changes in this century and many owners. During the Second World War it was a Municipal Maternity unit for difficult cases and after the war it was owned by Reckitt and Colman Ltd. as a residence for executives. In recent years it has become a residential home for the elderly. Tom Boothby, market gardener, worked the land to the rear of his cottage No.50 (to the left of Greystones) and later his son-in-law, John W. Lawson, used the premises as a dairy.

View dated 1903.

NORTH GATE, COTTINGHAM, "SCOTT" SERIES. No. 690.

Southwood Villa (No.86 South Street)

This house in South Street belonged to the Burgoyne and Egleston families, passing by 1789 to a Hull shipowner, Charles Shipman. Richard Farnill, Cottingham market gardener, bought it in 1797 and it passed to James Featherstone, Hull merchant in 1814, who bequeathed it on his death in 1822 to his son John. John Featherstone junior was bankrupt by 1831 and the liquidators sold the house to Edward Warner, solicitor of London. On his death in 1847 his son Edward acquired the property and by the end of the century the house was rebuilt.

It is possible that the much moved shipowner William Henry Heap Hutchinson may have lived there for a time, but the best remembered occupant must have been the redoubtable Madame Clapham, couturier and dress designer to the aristocracy including Queen Maude of Norway.

Southwood Villa at the turn of the century.

Elmtree House and grounds.

Elmtree House (Memorial Club) South Street

Built c.1820 on a 2½ acre site off South Street this fine house belonged to John Hebblewhite, Hull draper, who acquired the site in 1809, copyhold of the Powis manor. On his death in 1832, it passed by 1834 to Richard Wilson, a draper from Dudley (Worcs.) and he conveyed the property to John Clay, Hull merchant in 1843, who had it altered and enlarged in the 1860's.

The house was used as a hall of residence by the University College as an annexe to Needler Hall from October 1936 to June 1937 under the name of "New Hall". In 1937 the students removed to Westfield House and Elmtree House became a St. John's first aid post during wartime. It is now used as a clubhouse and headquarters of the Royal British Legion.

"Bainesse" during occupation in the 1930's by the Holtbys.

Bainesse (Holtby House) Thwaite Street

Situated on the outskirts of the village, this house is typical of the new villas erected in Cottingham by the new gentry, and affluent merchants of Hull, taking advantage of improved access to Hull via road and railway. Now a University Hall of residence known as Holtby House, it is best known for its association with Winifred Holtby, the celebrated authoress of "South Riding" and many other novels of local interest. Winifred's mother, Mrs. Alice Holtby, was the first woman to be made Alderman of the local county council and was most probably the model for Alderman Mrs. Beddows of the novel "South Riding". During the lifetime of the Holtbys the house was known as "Bainesse", and the name was changed to mark their association with the house.

Thwaite house as purchased by the University (by courtesy of the University of Hull).

Thwaite House (Thwaite Hall)

This house was erected by John Hentig (Hull merchant) in 1803 on land copyhold of the Rectory manor in part. He died in 1853 and afterwards the house was refaced and enlarged. David Wilson J.P. was there in 1872, when brother Charles was at Park House, but by 1879 David had moved to Park House. It was last privately occupied by Col. William Edward Goddard from c.1893 until its purchase by the University College of Hull on March 3rd, 1928 (£8,300), some months before the College opened. Now a women's Hall, it has been greatly extended, but the landscaped garden has been retained as the only remaining estate garden in Cottingham.

47

Thwaite lake and a portion of the gardens (by courtesy of the University of Hull).

Street Scenes in Cottingham

Hallgate, east end c.1903.

Hallgate

A view looking east, of the principal street in Cottingham, showing a block, mainly of shops, and probably dated c.1903. Notable features include a typical group of children, obviously aware of the camera, and behind them a horse drawn omnibus belonging to Herbert Hatfield, cab and omnibus owner at 121 Hallgate. The white barn with its end to the street and the adjoining house were demolished soon after, but the pharmacist's shop still remains, as do the shops on the right hand edge of the picture, although altered in appearance. Miss Lee had a wonderful toy shop here!

Hallgate (looking west)

This view of Hallgate is from the church and is from a postcard, date stamped 1906. The first shop was a pork butchers owned by Frank Hatfield and the next shop was the post office, registry and general store. The postmaster was Mr. Herbert J. Tadman, who was the pioneer photographer responsible for this picture. The white barn was reputed to be the registered meeting house for Cottingham's first Primitive Methodists before their church was built in King Street (North) in 1860. Mr. H. Hatfield's omnibus ran from this point before the days of the motor-bus and by 1913 the barn and white house in this picture were demolished and replaced by two shops for Mr. W. Pybus (Sartor House) and Mr. Cornelius Tutill, now a restaurant and Trustee Savings Bank respectively. There were two barbers near the corner with King Street (South); Mr. W.W. Knaggs and Mr. Richard Marshall, next door to each other! George Kirke was pharmacist and operated a lending library in the shop which has remained a pharmacy up to the present day with tastefully restored frontage.

A further view from a similar position showing developments by 1922. The motor car had arrived on the scene, hence the policeman on point duty at the cross roads, although Cottingham was soon to be one of the first urban councils to install traffic lights.

Hallgate

This view looking west from King Street corner is dated about 1904. The shops on the left hand side (Nos. 139 and 141) belonged to William Henry Clarke, confectioner, and Mrs. Dixon, druggist, respectively. No. 141 had been a druggist shop at least from the 1820's, when William Gunnee produced "Gunnee's Powders" for infants, extensively advertised in the Victorian press, a somewhat lethal compound containing white precipitate of mercury!

Across the street was Mr. Houseley, chimney sweep (see the sweep's brush above his name board), then a Georgian House called Ivy Leigh, followed by a contractor's yard (Mr. J. H. Wright) and the King William IV inn.

Soon Mr. John Henry Wright, contractor and entrepreneur, was to alter the scene on this side as shown in the next picture.

Hallgate, Cottingham.

About 1908 Mr. Wright decided to convert his work yard into shop premises and at the same time convert Ivy Leigh into a fine shop frontage, to house the new post office and the Cottingham offices of the London Joint Stock Bank. This view shows the changes involved in this part of Hallgate about 1922.

A view of Mr. J. H. Wright's contractor's yard before conversion, c.1905 (postcard stamped 1906). Mr. Wright stands in front of the Post office notice board (left hand figure) and the second person inside the yard is "Cabby" Kirby who drove the horse cab from King Street (North). The tall chimney in the background belonged to Thurloe's brewery at the rear of the public house and Mr. Bland's forge is the building at the rear.

This was the final result of Mr. Wright's conversion. There was a shop for C. J. Mudd and an office and entry to the yard beyond (now enshrined in modern parlance as "Mudd's Yard"). The Wrights had a fine flat over the shop in Palm Court style, with a verandah above the bay window jutting out from the roof. J. H. W. is here seen on the verandah shortly after completion. The verandah had to be removed by about 1920 as it became unsafe. These premises now belong to McLeish the bakers, and Mr. Hall, electrician, occupies the small shop which was Mr. Wright's office. Note the fine frontage to the London Joint Stock Bank premises, duplicated on the right hand side for Mr. H. J. Tadman's new post office. The old post office near the church was used to convert Hatfield's pork butchers into a double fronted shop (now the carpet shop).

Hallgate

Another view c.1912, showing the post office built into the frontage of Ivy Leigh for Mr. H. J. Tadman, postmaster and registrar (also photographer!). The London Joint Stock Bank, and the London City and Midland Bank, amalgamated and occupied Richard Marshall's old shop on the corner of King Street South by about 1913-14, as the modern Midland Bank. Next to the King William IV inn can be seen the tall building with a hoist, which was for Ness's the grain merchants, with the maltings to the rear.

Ness and Co.

This photograph shows Mrs. Ness, wearing a billycock hat at the warehouse door of the cornfactors. The lorry at the side is on its way to Thurloe's brewery and very faintly in this old photograph can be seen the flue-roof of the malt kiln.

The maltings were a very important factor in the development of brewing in Cottingham, as Thurloe's brewery served not only King Billy but also the Duke of Cumberland, (William Thurloe had been host to both inns) and possibly others. It comprised kiln, malt floor and storeroom. Falling into disuse after brewing ceased in the inter-war years, the upper malt floor, because of its great length, was used as a reception room for weddings etc; the Brocklesby family had acquired the buildings from Ness's estate in 1939. Falling completely into disrepair by the 1970's the maltings were completely demolished in 1977 to make way for development of the new Grandways complex.

This was the new face of Ness's building after its sale to Mr. Arthur Brocklesby in 1939, when he made a note on the back of this photograph to the effect that the whole property cost him £750. The present premises are used as a florist and gardening shop, undergoing further development (1988) to house pet foods etc.

Hallgate

Possibly the favourite view of Hallgate, looking East towards the church, dated about 1906.

On the right hand side the shop at the edge of the picture (No. 161) was R. Geddes, tailor; then at 159, Mr. Hutton, fruiterer and general store (later to become Mrs. D. Barker's toy and sweet shop and still in business under the ownership of her daughter, Mrs. Anne Ford). Wm. Isgate came next (157) with boot and shoe repairs; lower down Charles H. Tranmer, pork butcher (151), Charles Ashton, plumber (149) and Frank Pullan, butcher at 143.

When newly built, from a water-colour c.1880.

Hallgate Methodist Church

Built in 1878, it replaced a Wesleyan church formerly in Northgate near the Cross Keys Inn and at the rear of the present Cottingham Rifle Club. A friend of John Wesley, the prime founder of the Northgate building was Thomas Thompson, Hull banker, of Cottingham Castle. The Northgate building was extended, but was later sold as a steam laundry when the new church was built in Hallgate. The Wesleyans amalgamated with the Primitives in the mid 1930's and the Primitive Methodist church was vacated and sold to the Salvation Army who never used it as it was requisitioned in war years as a warehouse for Jarman and Flints. Of recent years the Hallgate building, although retaining its exterior intact, has undergone radical alterations internally to a two floor structure. Throughout the years the grounds to the frontage have altered.

Hallgate Methodist Church in the 1920's.

Beckbridge Farm c.1895 as occupied by the Lawsons.

Fussey's Corner, Hallgate

By association with a local Cottingham family, who ran a motor-bus service from Cottingham to Hull from this corner, at the junction of Beck Bank and Hallgate at its South west end.

The farm, known as Beckbridge Farm, was occupied by Mr. Henry Lawson and his family, cowkeepers and farmers. After Mr. Lawson's death, the family moved to Town End Farm at Skidby (c.1912) and the property was acquired by Mr. Tom Fussey who had recently purchased the bus service.

The house was demolished in the 1960's after futile attempts had been made to repair it, and the land to the rear has in recent times been developed and is known as "Victoria's Way".

Beckbridge Farm c.1935.

Wath House, Hallgate

Earlier known as "Applegarth" possibly because it was situated on the Applegarth of the Castle. It was for many years the residence of the Buttery family, monumental masons. The house was demolished with neighbouring property to make way for a modern development of flats.

Wath House c.1920.

One of the livery stables off Priory Road.

"Merry Hampton Stables"

In the previous view of Beckbridge Farm in 1895 may be seen a long low building in the background adjoining Arlington Villas. This was one of the stables owned by Mr. John Crowther Metcalf Harrison, who was a breeder of racehorses. In 1884 he handed over the stables to his son John Simons Harrison, who bought a yearling at Doncaster for 3,100 guineas (£3,255). This proved to be a good bargain as the horse, "Merry Hampton" was entered for the Derby of 1887 and won easily. John Simons Harrison carried on the livery stables for fifty years, expanding into the area of what is now Priory Road. The stables in the Hallgate area occupied part of the estate of Kingtree House and approached by way of Newgate Street (now the entrance to Kingtree Avenue).

George Street, Hallgate side.

George Street

This street, named after George Knowsley, owner of the Grange, who created it in lieu of the ancient right of way through the castle grounds, which he had purchased in part to extend his boundaries. It dips to one of the lowest levels in the village leading to drainage problems when Keldgate springs flow. In June 1912 the area was almost completely flooded by a cloudburst. There has been much development recently in this area despite drainage problems on the site at Crescent Street, off George Street.

George Street, Northgate entrance.

Floods in George Street - Crescent Street,
June 1912.

West End Road

At the turn of the century a tree-lined country road leading to Eppleworth road and Skidby, with Westfield House standing alone at the entrance and the Dene at the rear. Development took place in the mid 1930's, with the building of houses, so that now it resembles any other urban road of inter-war years.

West End Road c.1900.

West End Road mid 1930's. Many of the original trees remain (left hand side of this photograph).

64

West Green

This was most probably the earliest and only true "green" in Cottingham, for as far as is known "Market Green" was never grassed. It is likely that the original market licensed by King John, was held here, and was not moved to Market Green until much later.

West Green, Cottingham.

A view of West Green c.1910, showing a Boer War cannon, one of two acquired by Cottingham in 1904. Cottages originally lined the entrance to Finkle Street, now gone, and the old Blue Bell Inn was the most important house!

The Blue Bell Inn c.1906. Samuel Mears, innkeeper and also pig breeder in nearby
Finkle Street.

Northgate. *Click-em-in*

Click-em-inn in its original form.

This was the "gata" or street running on the northern side of Cottingham, leading to the common land at its eastern end. Just two years ago the immediate point of interest on entering Northgate from the west was a small semi-derelict cottage set at a slight angle to the road. This was totally demolished and some of the old bricks used in the erection of a much larger structure with the totally inappropriate name of "Toll Cottage" (there never was one!). Legend has it that the original cottage was a small ale house — too small to be described as an inn, but many small cottages in the 17-18th centuries provided ale for the thirsty traveller. To many local inhabitants it bore the name "Click-em-in(n)", of dubious derivation. The angle at which this was set to the road possibly followed the line of the old road through the manor grounds.

Northgate from the end of George Street

This picture is dated about 1910, from a position where the gates to the present King George V playing fields are situated. There were two blocks of fine houses on the left hand side, including Mr. Frank Pullan's abattoir, and a block of small cottages called Mount Pleasant. Beyond these can be seen a large building wreathed in steam; this was the steam laundry in the old Wesleyan church. The wall on the right hand side encloses two properties:- Beech House (Beech Tree House) No. 191 and Northfields (now Needler Hall).

Northgate. The Cross Keys

At its junction with King Street (north), the latter originally known as "Broad Lane", this most interesting section of Northgate is shown in old photographs.

This view is dated 1906 (date stamp) and shows the Cross Keys Inn (Mrs. Mary E. Cockerline) as part of a terraced row of Cottages. The archway led through into a close of cottages with the official name of "Providence Place", but known in the vernacular as "Sweeps Square". The general store owned by Mrs. Brown also served as an "off licence" to the Cross Keys and remained in this capacity (later in the Wigby family) for many years. It closed for a short time in the 1980's, but has opened again since 1986. The view has changed a little by 1922, particularly in respect of the refurbishment of the Cross Keys, with larger windows and the rendering of the old brick work.

There was a long line of Cottages on the left hand side including Mrs. Hall's fish and chip shop. Mr. Arthur

Northgate and Cross Keys 1906.

Brocklesby had a greengrocer cum general store in a yard off the street and the Longbones had a lorry service. These cottages ended at Yokefleet (later, York House) and there was an orchard belonging to Yokefleet where the terrace block Nos. 62 to 74 now stand before arriving at Millbeck Lane. On the other side of the road outstanding features were a garage, selling "Russian Oil Products" and a cottage, the home of Mr. W.E. Wright, at 69 Northgate — noteworthy as the birthplace of Mr. Alec Wright, a local artist who moved to Stokesley (N. Yorks) and was a regular artist to "the Dalesman" and other periodicals. His sister Ellen, later Mrs. Ellen Brace, became a local historian, largely responsible for the restoration of Gainsborough Old Hall, one of the finest timbered halls left in England.

Then came the Salvation Army hall, which was totally destroyed by fire in 1958 and as a result they acquired new premises on the site of the old Wesleyan Church near the present Cottingham Rifle Club.

The next large house belonged to Mr. W. Fewster, blacksmith, at No. 87; later on the forge passed to Mr. John Turner, blacksmith there for many years until the house and forge disappeared in the heady days of the 1960's rush of development.

Northgate and Cross Keys 1922.

Northgate from Mill Beck Lane c.1898

A view of Northgate including Mr. Tom Boothby's cottage (No. 50), Greystones (No. 46), and cottages to Millhouse Woods Lane. Beyond the trees there was a long low building which housed the fire engine of 1887. Northgate was quite a rural lane as shown by the number of children in the street and the cows being driven back, probably to No. 50.

Looking the other way up Northgate from Priory Cottage, date about 1910. Before 1900 the house near the first lamp post was a single storey cottage, but here it is seen to have an extension upwards. The string course shows the level of the pre-1900 roof line.

NORTHGATE, COTTINGHAM.

Railway crossing
c.1920.

Railway Crossing, Northgate

This crossing has seen many changes during the years, particularly in the years 1970-1988. This picture is dated about 1920 and shows the old gates and Cottingham North signal box, which was removed at the end of 1987 and has gone to Hull Transport Museum. Now the gates are of modern drop-down type, controlled by television from Beverley.

New Village Road

As a result of the 1766 enclosure plan a portion of land allocated to Cottingham Church, was let out in strips to the poor of the parish in lieu of poor relief, in the hope that they would be able to maintain a living for their families. Originally known as "paupers' gardens" the settlement eventually received the more acceptable appellation of "New Village".

This view shows the road down to the New Village and its eventual junction to Hull Road.

The shop on the right hand side in the middle distance belonged to Mr. Leonard Thompson, who also owned a shop on the corner of King Street (north). Mr. Thompson, a local councillor, did much for Cottingham as a diligent seeker after village rights and also as local historian and conserver of old material which would almost certainly have been destroyed. Dated c.1910.

The cottages in Endyke Lane, constructed by the poor, on land rented from the church. Thomas Thompson of Cottingham Castle was mainly responsible for the scheme.

King Street and Market Green

King Street runs south to north across the village, skirting the Market Green on its way. Originally the northern portion was known as Broad Lane and earlier directories describe it thus. For convenience the two portions may be designated King Street (south) from South Street to Hallgate, and King Street (north) from Hallgate to Northgate.

King Street (south) and Market Green figure very prominently in postcards, showing the changes between about 1885 and 1922. At earlier times artists' impressions, for example a view by Frith, of Market Green, show that the western side of the square was occupied by cottages and a variety of trade establishments. There was Sammy Green's forge, a saddler's workshop and Frith's coach painting shop, where the Council offices now stand. The Council offices were opened by Dr. George Watson, Medical Officer of Health, in 1909 and the present Civic Hall is a post-war building replacing the cottages. On the east side of King Street,

opposite to Finkle Street, a block of shops, including a pharmacist, building society, shoe shop etc., ending with a supermarket (Willis), all occupy the area where Kingtree House and stables stood. The long building now Hutchinson's shop and lately the Gas Company showrooms was originally built as a cinema, known as the "Regent" (1912, manager Arthur Spinks). Between 1920-22 it was used by Mr. Fred Singleton as a pearl button factory. From 1922-24 it was the "Coliseum" and by 1925 the "Imperial" (manger W. H. Roberts). Originally a line of cottages stood there, seen in an early postcard. The Duke of Cumberland saw changes too; earlier photographs, show it covered with a creeper, then it changes to bare brick about 1916 and later it is plaster rendered in its last guise. Originally there were three public houses in King Street: the Duke of Cumberland, then the "Angel" and finally the "Tiger". The Angel Inn after the First World War eventually became the headquarters of the British Legion before it moved to the present Memorial Club.

KING STREET—COTTINGHAM.

King Street (south) from South Street corner

The archway on the right hand side led to a small square containing the forge of Mr. Henry Humble and known as "Casson's Yard", often facetiously referred to as "Leicester Square". The building jutting out from Finkle Street entrance, opposite the large tree, was the Cottingham Literary and Reading Room, demolished in the mid 1960's. On the opposite side of Finkle Street, adjoining the present Post Office, stood a plain Georgian building known as King Street Rooms, demolished some ten years later. This building was a useful asset to all village life as a meeting hall, exhibition hall, jumble sale venue, etc., and has been sadly missed since its replacement by flats and shops. On the edge of Market Green there were also "infill" cottages and a shoe repair shop, all demolished in the 1960's.

A gathering of children in fancy dress costume outside the Reading Room c.1939.

Market Green and King Street c.1898 with children in the street, the "Duke" with creeper, and the "Angel" Inn.

A similar view but dated 1922-24 showing the "Coliseum" cinema, the Duke of Cumberland and a motor bus.

KING STREET. COTTINGHAM

King Street Rooms originally the "National School" before the building of the "Board School" in Hallgate. Taken shortly before demolition this photograph shows the entrance to the school on the extreme left of the picture.

King Street c.1885.

King Street Corner (from Hallgate)

This postcard shows one of the most popular views of Cottingham dated c.1885, with the ubiquitous crowd of children posing for their photographs! It shows three public houses; the "Tiger", "Angel" and Duke of Cumberland; King Tree House stables, some fine shops and infill cottages on the Green. The hand-cart bears the name "Brown", belonging to the shop in Northgate and it is possible that the boy in charge could by Frank Wigby, who eventually took over the shop.

Thwaite Street Crossing

A view of Thwaite railway crossing, about 1900, showing the signal cabin. The farm over the crossing has now been replaced by the Beechdale development including a block of flats, described by an eminent local historian as an excellent example of shoe-box architecture!

Thwaite Street from Beck Bank Corner c.1905

At this time Thwaite Street had two inns, the Railway Hotel (Mr. Brian Lazenby) and the Duke of York (Alfred Padley). The Railway Hotel survived into the early 1960's when it was demolished and rebuilt on the corner of Beck Bank. The Duke of York never seemed to flourish and was demolished in the 1930's. Note the advertisement for the Grand Theatre in Hull showing "The Merry Widow".

Reproduced by courtesy of the Hull Daily Mail.

Beck Bank.

Dated 1898, this picture shows the beck on its way to the Snuff Mill and a street lined with cottages, with a large house belonging to the Fusseys.

Reproduced by courtesy of the Hull Daily Mail.

The Railway Station

The Hull to Bridlington line was opened in 1846 with a station at Cottingham, an event which must have dealt a death blow to the toll house and turnpike road to Cottingham, which had been opened in 1770. Here is seen Cottingham station in 1913, before the building of the exterior ticket office. Many of the features still survive, but the goods shed and wagon shed are defunct and the island goods platform and gantry signal have gone.

A steam train is passing the signal box on its way to Hull. The cannon shown here arrived in Cottingham in 1904 as a memento of the Boer War, and remained here until the early 1930's. The other cannon which arrived with it was placed on West Green.

A steam train to Hull in the early days of British Railways after nationalisation. The late Mr. Harold Burton, chief porter for many years and (unofficial) gardener to the station, is the figure on the right near the flower bed.

Motor Transport

Cottingham entered the motor transport age in the 1910-1920's. There had been a horse bus service from Hallgate near the church and by 1920 a regular bus service started. There are records of a "Swift" motor bus service with a depot in Northgate, which was later turned into a garage owned by the Rapers. This service seems to have lasted from 1922-1924 with two buses, "Swift" and "Swallow".

Fusseys and the Kingston bus service ran buses at half hourly intervals between Paragon Street, Hull and Cottingham Market Green at four old pence a trip (less than 2p). The intervals were arranged to give a quarter hour service from 7.00 a.m. to 10.45 p.m. Motor lorries carried produce to Hull markets and further afield and there were hauliers for furniture etc. Some of the wealthier families, for example, the Rollits and Grotrians, had chauffeur-driven private motor cars.

Cottingham Haulage Contractors c.1922.

Old solid tyred motor bus leaves Cottingham Green 1924.

Motor car belonging to Sir Arthur Rollit of Browsholme with his chauffeur.

A very early motor bus belonging to East Yorkshire Motor Company.

Cottingham Personalities

Mr. John Turner

A much loved figure in Cottingham, John originally had a forge in Fewster's yard off Northgate, vacating these premises during the 1960's shortly before demolition. He built a new forge in Millhouse Woods Lane near his own house, but once again had to leave this to make way for the erection of Mr. Jaram's house. John then settled in a yard off Dunswell Road near its junction with Northmoor Lane, but soon a group of inhabitants newly settled in new bungalows began to complain to the council of "noise and smell" and caused an eviction order to be executed. However, an immediate petition championed by the late Mr. H. Wright, local tomato and potato grower, and signed by many hundreds of local people ensured reversal of the order and John continued to work there until his retirement. He died in 1979, sadly missed by all his friends. The whole story was covered by the Hull Daily Mail on May 17th, 1972 and their photographer produced this truly delightful picture of John at work.

Photo by courtesy of Hull Daily Mail.

Mr. John William Lawson

Son of Mr. Henry Lawson of Beck Bridge Farm, Hallgate, born on 18th November, 1888, married Miss Harriet Boothby on 25th February, 1915, and settled at No. 50 Northgate, on a small-holding formerly owned by Tom Boothby. Mr. Lawson was a dairy farmer and a well known figure in Cottingham, for many years a committee member for the Cottingham Horse Show executive. In this photograph he is seen delivering milk at a bungalow in Dunswell Road, with horse Tommy. He died, aged 71 years, in November 1959.

Mr. Harry Atkinson

A member of a very well known local family, Mr. Atkinson began to work for Mr. John William Lawson on his farm at No. 50 Northgate as a school leaver and remained with him for the rest of his life. A truly rural worker, farming was his whole life and in this photograph he is shown in Park Lane, his favourite territory, riding "Peggy" and leading "Violet". It is interesting to note that he rode side-saddle in this picture, the usual mode used by farm workers. He died in 1960, aged 55 years.

George Henry Watson, L.S.A.

A prominent figure in Cottingham Society, Dr. Watson was Medical Officer to the Cottingham Urban District Council for many years, living at No. 8 Hallgate, now known as "Kings-winford". Here he is seen with his wife at the official opening of the new Council Offices on Market Green in 1909.

Charles Henry Wilson, 1st Baron Nunburnholme 1833-1907

The son of Thomas Wilson and Susannah (nee West), he spent his earlier years at Park House in Northgate; he joined his father in the shipping firm, eventually acquiring control of the Company. He soon built the firm into the major shipping line in the country and was elevated to the peerage in 1905. In this photograph he is seen in his younger days with his wife Florence Jane Helen, elder daughter of Colonel William Henry Charles Wellesley, nephew of the Duke of Wellington. They are here photographed at Park House, long before removing to Warter Priory. Charles Wilson later built "The Bungalow" in Thwaite Street (now Cleminson Hall) as a second residence in Cottingham to his seat at Warter Priory.

Charles Henry Wilson and his wife at Park House.

Frank Pullan, Butcher, Hallgate

Probably the oldest surviving shop in Cottingham to remain in the same family; the exterior of this shop has changed little over the years. The young man handling the prime beef specimen in the street was Mr. Ernest Downes and the older person in the shop door way was Mr. Frank Pullan, grandfather of the present Mr. Frank Pullan, who now owns the business. This picture dates about 1912.

Winifred and Alice Holtby

Winifred and Alice Holtby at Bainesse, March 1934. Picture by courtesy of Miss Jill Crowther, B.A. of the Hull Local History Library.

Winifred Holtby was born on June 23rd, 1898 at Rudston House to David and Alice Holtby, where David farmed at Rudston, North Yorkshire. Following agricultural labour problems during the war years, the family left Rudston in 1918 and settled in Cottingham at "Bainesse" in Thwaite Street. Winifred had entered Somerville College, Oxford, to read history but her work was interrupted by the war until 1919 when she re-entered Oxford and took an upper second honours degree — one of the first batch of women to be allowed a degree from Oxford following alterations in Oxford University regulations. She had met Vera Brittain at Somerville and formed a firm friendship, the subject of the latter's book after Winifred's death, "Testament of Friendship". Winifred and Vera shared a flat in London from 1922 when Winifred's first novel "Anderby Wold" was written and published. Winifred paid visits to Cottingham at Bainesse and took a limited part in the social life of the village, although she did not really like Cottingham, never forgetting her love of Rudston. Her second novel, "The Crowded Street" (1924) appears to have been based on her experiences in Cottingham and much of Winifred is to be found in her heroine "Muriel Hammond".

Her father David died at Bainesse following bronchitis on March 9th, 1933 and her mother Alice had entered local government, eventually to become the first woman Alderman on the East Yorkshire County Council. She was to be the model for Alderman Mrs. Beddows in Winifred's most famous novel, "South Riding". Winifred's life was full and eventful and she achieved much, although alas it was to be pitifully short, for she died of kidney failure on September 29th, 1935. Her last novel was published after her death by her life-long friend Vera Brittain. She was buried at Rudston amongst her own folk with this epitaph:-

> "God give me work
> Till my life shall end;
> And life
> Till my work is done".

Mr. J. B. Boynton and Mr. F. Pecket

An informal "snap" of two Cottingham stalwarts, "Johnny" Boynton on the left and Fred Pecket on the right, standing outside the girls' school in Hallgate. Johnny Boynton was described in the directories at the turn of the century as "foreman at the gas works" and later as journeyman gas fitter and plumber, but his popular name was "Johnny come tomorrow" because when requested to do a job of work he would almost invariably reply, "I'll come tomorrow"! Fred Pecket was a very popular caretaker at the Hallgate school for many years and lived in George Street.

Mr. Fred Nalton

A very popular figure in Cottingham, Mr. Nalton started out his career as a telegraph boy to Mr. H. J. Tadman at the post office in Cottingham. He is seen standing in the doorway of the second post office in Hallgate in his uniform. Later to spend his life in the post office service, he was also an indefatigable worker for the church and acted as verger in his retirement for many years, before his death.

Mr. John Henry Wright

Builder, contractor and entrepreneur, Mr. Wright was an energetic person, responsible for much change in the appearance of Hallgate in the Edwardian era. Previous pictures have shown the extent of these changes; this view shows one of his cabs and two carts outside the Primitive Methodist Church in King Street (North). Mr. Wright had an entrance to his works premises near this point in King Street and the second view is of a gathering of his workforce in the work-yard. Mr. Wright is standing near the extreme left of this picture.

King Street Primitive Methodist Church with Mr. J. H. Wright beside the horse-cab.

Mr. J. H. Wright and work-force in the builders' yard.

The National United Order of Free Gardeners

This Friendly Society was founded in 1820 and was intended as a type of insurance against illness and the prospect of loss of work in the days long before the advent of Social Services. Cottingham had a branch which eventually adopted the name "C. H. Wilson Lodge", with all the requisite regalia. This rally in 1906 shows a gathering of officials, with Mr. Hubert Humble, farrier of King Street holding the Society's emblem: a pair of clasped hands mounted on a pedestal.

Haltemprice Urban District Council

On 1st April, 1935 in order to combat the threat of "take-over" by the encroaching county of Kingston Upon Hull, a number of local parish councils amalgamated to produce one collective authority to be known as "Haltemprice", derived from the old name of the Priory "Alta Prise". This photograph is one of the last group of members of the old Cottingham Urban District Council taken in March 1934.

The Cottingham Travellers

For very many years a common sight in Northgate was the passage of the Travellers or Gypsies to their site in the chalk pits on Harland Way. This photograph was taken in 1956 and the scene was soon to be a memory with the advent of motor-caravans and eventually the establishment of permanent sites in Cottingham for the Gypsies.

Cottingham Horse Show Committee, 1930

Standing left to right:-
F. Boynton (Hon. Sec.); G. Gardham (Chairman); J. W. Lawson; J. Fern; W. Scott.
A. Robinson; Mr. Palmer; A. Palmer; J. Elvidge; Mr. Lawnes; Mr. Witty;......?
Seated:- left to right
A. Turner; Mr. Ridley (Vet); J. Byass; H. Samman; Dr. Jackson.

Cottingham has enjoyed successful Horse Shows during the whole of this century and earlier, and has seen many of the best known show jumpers over the years. This photograph is one of the Executive Committee, headed by the President Dr. T. C. Jackson, an eminent local solictor.